About One Earth Books

During its nearly one hundred years of educating the public about environmental issues, the National Audubon Society has rarely achieved anything as important as reaching out to the world's young people, the voices of tomorrow. For Audubon and its 600,000 members, nothing is so crucial as ensuring that those voices speak in the future on behalf of wildlife.

Audubon reaches out to people in many ways—through its nationwide system of wildlife sanctuaries, through research vital to helping set the nation's environmental policy, through lobbying for sound conservation laws, through television documentaries and fact-based dramatic films, through *Audubon* magazine and computer software, and through ecology workshops for adults and Audubon Adventures clubs in school classrooms. Each of these is critical to reaching a large audience. And now, with the Audubon One Earth books, the environmental community can speak to the young minds in our citizenry.

Aubudon is proud to publish One Earth in cooperation with Delacorte Press. In addition to bringing new information and experiences to young readers, these books will instill in them a fundamental concern for the environment and its decline at the hands of humanity. They will also, it is hoped, stimulate an undying interest in the natural world that will empower young people, as they mature, to protect the world's natural wonders for themselves and for future generations.

We at Audubon hope you will enjoy the One Earth books and that you will find in them an inspiration for joining our earth-saving mission. Young people are the hope for our future.

Christopher N. Palmer
Executive Editor
President, National Audubon
Society Productions

ONE EARTH

SAVE OUR PRAIRIES AND GRASSLANDS

RON HIRSCHI

Photographs by Erwin and Peggy Bauer

National
Audubon
Society

DELACORTE PRESS/NEW YORK

If you would like to receive more information about the
National Audubon Society write to:

National Audubon Society, Membership Department,
700 Broadway, New York, New York 10003

Executive Editor: Christopher N. Palmer

Published by
Delacorte Press
Bantam Doubleday Dell Publishing Group, Inc.
1540 Broadway
New York, New York 10036

Library of Congress Cataloging in Publication Data

Hirschi, Ron.
 Save our prairies and grasslands / by Ron Hirschi ; photographs by Erwin and Peggy Bauer.
   p.   cm.
 "An Audubon one earth book."
 Includes index.
 ISBN 0-385-31149-4.—ISBN 0-385-31199-0 (pbk.)
 1. Prairie ecology—United States—Juvenile literature.
2. Prairies—United States—Juvenile literature.   3. Prairie
conservation—United States—Juvenile literature.   4. Grassland
ecology—United   States—Juvenile   literature.   5.   Grasslands—United   States—Juvenile
literature.   [1. Prairies.   2. Prairie ecology.
3. Grasslands.   4. Grassland ecology.   5. Ecology.]   I. Bauer,
Erwin A.   II. Bauer, Peggy.   III. Title.
QH104.H55   1994
574.5'2643—dc20   93-4985   CIP   AC

This edition is published simultaneously in a
Delacorte Press hardcover edition and a Delacorte
Press trade paperback edition.

Manufactured in the United States of America

March 1994

10 9 8 7 6 5 4 3 2 1

For Ted Turner
with thanks
for your vision

Contents

Grasslands are scattered throughout the United States, but major prairie regions—areas dominated by grasses and wildflowers—carpet whole regions of our country. There are essentially three kinds of prairies in the United States—shortgrass, midgrass, and tallgrass. When traveling the country from west to east you can actually see one kind of prairie give way to the next. Shortgrass prairies define an enormous chunk of land within and just east of the Rocky Mountains. As you reach parts of the Dakotas, Colorado, Wyoming, and Nebraska, midgrass prairies converge. Eventually, in the Midwest, tallgrass prairie habitat takes over. However, not much is left of the spectacular oceans of tallgrass that once marked Nebraska, Illinois, Indiana, and other midwestern states. Many have been replaced by farms.

American prairies have always supported an incredibly wealthy agricultural industry. Native American farmers and hunters harvested some of the earth's most plentiful and important plant and animal crops from the grasslands for centuries. Today's farmers grow almost enough food on this land to feed the entire world. But the switch from the Native American's use of the prairies to our current agricultural system has come at great cost. Agricultural chemicals have polluted groundwater, lakes, and rivers throughout the prairie states. Wildlife populations have disappeared, and the soil has been depleted of valuable nutrients.

In the West, particularly in and around the Rocky Mountains, where the lower-growing prairie grasslands are not quite as valuable for farming because crops don't grow as well at 5,000 feet, shortgrass prairies have been spared some of the insults eastern tallgrass regions have endured. So what is it about tallgrass prairie areas that makes them so much better for farming?

Soil. Water. Fire. That's right. These three ingredients play a major role in making prairie ecosystems so attractive to farmers. Generally, deeper soil and heavier rainfalls occur in the tallgrass regions. And natural fire once ensured that grasses would dominate. For centuries, fires set by Native Americans and natural fires swept across the land, burning young trees so that grasses could stay in charge. It was only when people began to control fires by putting them out too quickly that trees began to sneak out onto the prairie. In the past, when trees were kept to a minimum by natural fire, prairie regions were easier to plow and therefore more inviting to farmers than other habitats.

Today, every prairie has some trees. When sprinkled throughout the grasslands, they provide valuable habitat for many animals. Water in many forms can also be found in most prairies. Wetlands form in low-lying areas, and rivers and streams flow through the prairies, offering yet another habitat for wildlife. In fact, most waterfowl are born in prairie wetlands.

Now that you have a general picture of prairies as they once were, and of prairies as they currently exist, let us begin a journey through the prairies and grasslands of the United States for an even closer look. Our first visit will be to the western landscape where our only vast prairies still remain—the shortgrass prairies.

SAVE OUR PRAIRIES AND GRASSLANDS

Shortgrass Prairies

If you travel east from just about anywhere on the West Coast of the United States, you will bump into the Rocky Mountains. The western slopes of these massive mountains are green with aspen, larch, fir, and pine trees. Snowfall and rainfall are heavy, though here and there you find a valley protected from the weather, where the land is drier. By contrast, once you cross over the mountains and drop down onto the eastern slopes of the Rockies, dry land is all you see.

Here the trees disappear, and the land becomes a beautiful bluish, silver green. Sagebrush is scattered across many hills, but others are dominated by grasses and prairie wildflowers. This shortgrass prairie landscape covers much of eastern Montana, then cuts south through eastern Wyoming, Colorado, and New Mexico. It also includes portions of western Nebraska, Kansas, and Texas.

Although not all the shortgrass prairies have been altered by the plow, they have been changed in other ways. Cattle grazing, irrigation, and the introduction of nonnative plants have affected much of the land. Nevertheless, shortgrass prairies are the least changed of the major American grasslands. Taller grasses and wildflowers are still scattered throughout this region, but the dominant species include two of our smallest grasses—buffalo grass and blue grama.

1

Buffalo Grass

It might be hard for you to get excited about grass. It isn't cuddly or cute, it doesn't run or fly, nor does it sing songs. But buffalo grass, as tough as an NFL linebacker, spreads a special kind of beauty across the prairie.

Buffalo, or bison, like to eat this grass. That's how it got its name. The enormous mammal and tiny grass share more than a name, though—they also share a unique relationship. Bison kick up a lot of ground as they graze, roll, or run. Their hooves are sharp, and they can lay bare large areas. This is especially true in wallows, which are dips in the ground created when bison roll in the mud or dusty ground to scratch their backs or to rid themselves of shedding hair or biting insects.

But buffalo grass can restore wallows and other bare ground almost as fast as the bison wear it down. It does this by spreading little arms of grass across the surface of the ground. These projectiles are known as stolons, and they can grow as fast as two inches per day. The stolons spread rapidly, sprouting tufts of new grass. Before long, mats of buffalo grass are ready for the next round of bison grazing.

In the days before we slaughtered the bison, buffalo grass went through this cycle of growing, getting knocked down, then growing again. Buffalo herds moved through the prairies, feeding until it was time to move on. The grass offered food for millions of bison, then grew back again as surely as the seasons came and went.

The big problem for grasslands and prairie ecosystems today is the division of land into sections. Cattle and sheep, unlike wild bison, are confined behind barbed wire fences that cut the prairie into small squares of land. Forced to roam in a confined area, the domestic livestock do not give the land a chance to renew itself, as the migratory bison once did.

Grasses can withstand a great deal of trampling, but they

ROOTS RUN DEEP

Roots of prairie grasses run deep into the soil, holding firm and collecting moisture. This moisture can be hard to find in many years, especially on shortgrass prairies where rainfall is far lower than in other areas. It is so low, in fact, that cactus commonly grow among the other prairie plants.

The leaves of buffalo grass reach only five inches above the ground, but the roots extend four feet underground—that's more than ten times the growth underground than above the surface.

must have a chance to sprout again. In the past, bison, pronghorn, elk, and other grazing animals moved through an area, then went on to new feeding grounds. By the time they returned, plants had recovered. Since animals are no longer free to roam and return, the prairie is beaten to death.

Buffalo even help replant grass. Buffalo grass seeds, which look like tiny burrs, hook onto a bison's matted fur, allowing them to hitch a ride across the prairie. As bison travel from place to place, they reseed the buffalo grass.

Actually, buffalo grass lawns are becoming very popular throughout the West. Adapted to dry conditions, they can thrive with small amounts of moisture. Millions of gallons of water could be saved if large numbers of homeowners planted this grass, as it requires very little water to grow. And buffalo grass's dense, beautiful carpet grows to be only five inches high. This means little mowing for homeowners, and also means the conservation of lawn mower gas and oil, which contribute greatly to air and water pollution.

A more natural lawn can be created by mixing buffalo grass with blue grama. This combination is naturally common in the shortgrass prairies stretching from Montana to Texas. The buffalo and blue grama lawns are tough, perhaps because

LAWN NOT

Step outside almost any house, school, or other building in America, and lawn spreads before you. It's so common, so abundant, and so much a part of our everyday life that most of us don't even think about it—until you have to mow, water, or feed it.

Americans spend millions of dollars manicuring their lawns. If the lawns sprout weeds or undesirable grasses, people poison them with gallons of chemicals. This poison then washes into rivers and streams, lakes and oceans.

A natural grassland could be growing where your perfect lawn now stands. A mixture of wildflowers and grass, that lawn could still be mowed for a volleyball game or croquet match. If the right grasses are chosen, the lawn doesn't even have to be mowed, watered, or fed. Native and tough, grasses like buffalo grass and blue grama grow only a few inches high and rarely need watering.

So why are we still growing unnatural lawns if alternatives exist that help save water and eliminate the need for chemicals? It may be that lawns, mowers, chemicals, and landscaping are big business. But at one time, the making and selling of wagons, harnesses, and wooden wheels was also big business. Maybe it is time lawns went the same way—back to the ways of a simpler era that were gentler on the environment.

of their long history of tolerating bison hooves. They need very little water and no fertilizer, insecticides, or fungicides.

Buffalo grass seeds are available today from many prairie grass and wildflower companies. By planting them, you may not encourage the return of millions of bison, but you can create a small, highly significant habitat. If enough people converted their lawns to small prairies, the water quality of streams, lakes, and wetlands would improve. Write to Stock Seed Farms, R.R. #1, Box 112, Murdock, Nebraska 68407, for seed information. Talk to your parents or your school officials about the possibility of creating a prairie lawn, and you'll be doing your part to help save the earth.

4

Prairie Dogs

A million of almost anything, except maybe stars, is tough to imagine. But 100 million is even more difficult, especially if they are all in one place. At one time, in Texas, there were 400 million prairie dogs, which were not scattered across the prairie as you might think, but were actually concentrated in one prairie dog town.

Prairie dogs live in families within towns not unlike our own. They watch out for one another, sit at the entrance to their burrows, and call out to one another if danger approaches. Beneath the ground, they live in condominiumlike dwellings. They build soft nests of grass as beds where young are born.

Knowing how many prairie dogs once existed makes it difficult to believe that we have driven them from so many areas. Millions ranged throughout the shortgrass prairies from Texas northward. When the bison herds were gone, ranchers moved their cattle onto the prairie. Since prairie dogs ate the grasses and plants, the ranchers believed they were competition for their livestock, and they began to shoot or gas them in their burrows. They even killed them by introducing the deadly disease bubonic plague into their colonies.

Today we know that because of their burrowing, the prairie dog actually improves the soil. Recent research has shown that cattle grow faster on land inhabited by prairie dogs than in areas where they have been removed. This is really no surprise when you consider that bison and prairie dogs lived together for many centuries. They both helped maintain, not destroy, the grassland by digging, burrowing, and trampling plants like buffalo grass, and then moving on, allowing them to resprout.

Ironically, ranchers continue to despise prairie dogs because of the burrows they dig. Throughout the West, prairie dogs are referred to as "gophers" and "varmints," and they are

5

Prairie dogs live together in large communities, and greetings between two individuals can be a lot like those between two people. Sometimes the greeting is just a friendly scratch on the back. Other times prairie dogs hug. They also do something quite sweet—prairie dogs seem to kiss. They embrace, and they touch their lips to one another, just like a kiss.

The kiss of the prairie dog is thought to be a way they identify one another. It helps one prairie dog let another one know it is recognized as part of the colony. A handshake among friends, the kiss reassures that prairie dogs are a part of the same community.

Prairie dog kissing and other close encounters are more common in one of the two prairie dog species than in the other. For instance, the white-tailed prairie dogs are not as community oriented as their relatives, the black-tailed prairie dogs. Black-tailed prairie dogs form enormous towns with millions of inhabitants.

If you ever visit a prairie dog town, watch for their kissing. Listen closely, too. Prairie dogs are highly vocal and communicate with one another about their concerns in the colonies. If one dog spots a golden eagle, coyote, or hawk, the others soon know that danger is near by the sound of the prairie dog's squeal.

routinely killed in every state in which they live. A small Colorado town actually celebrates a summer festival during which prairie dogs are shot. The prairie dog population has declined so drastically that one of its major predators, the black-footed ferret, has become the rarest mammal in North America.

Black-footed Ferrets

Black-footed ferrets are the sleek masked raiders of prairie dog towns. Life was good for these quick and efficient predators for many centuries. When prairie dogs numbered in the millions, they had lots of food. They even made their burrows in holes dug for them by their prey.

Black-footed ferrets once ranged from Alberta and British Columbia in the north to Texas and New Mexico in the south. At the turn of the century, when the western prairie dogs were killed in vast numbers, the ferrets began to disappear, too. They came very close to extinction.

Then, in 1964, when the prairie dog population increased in South Dakota, a very small ferret colony was discovered in the southwestern corner of the state. Biologists studied them taking some into care as part of a captive-breeding program. Although the ferrets in this area did not survive for very long, scientists were able to learn a lot by working with them. When a new group of ferrets was found near the small town of Meeteetse, Wyoming, in 1981, this earlier research enabled a new team of scientists to initiate recovery efforts for the endangered ferrets.

The wild ferrets in the Meeteetse area were watched closely as their population was counted. In 1984, there were an estimated 129 individuals. When the numbers suddenly dropped one year later, biologists captured 6 ferrets in an attempt to create a captive-breeding population. Unfortunately, canine distemper, a disease that is fatal to ferrets, spread through the captive population, and all of them died.

Despite this setback, 18 more ferrets were captured between 1986 and 1987. This time the captives lived, and their breeding has been successful.

In the fall of 1991, a total of 49 ferrets were set free in the Shirley Basin area of Wyoming in the first of several release efforts. At least 50 more will be added to that population each year and to other populations in Montana. These numbers are needed to help the animals firmly establish themselves in the area. Already several released ferrets have been killed by coyotes or badgers. Others have shown signs of stress due to lack of food or water. But efforts continue.

PRAIRIE PREDATORS

Running to capture your prey out in the open prairie is not an easy thing to do, and many prairie predators have evolved some unique ways to catch enough food to eat. They also share life-style habits peculiar to animals of open environments.

The burrowing owl and the badger, for example, both live underground. The burrowing owl nests in prairie dog burrows, making it the only member of its kind to use an underground living space. The badger also lives in prairie dog or ground squirrel holes, or it digs one of its own. More often, the badger digs to catch its small-mammal prey. Burrowing owls use wing power to catch insects, small mammals, and birds.

Coyotes are stealthy when stalking their prey. They walk slowly, listening, then leaping to snatch a meadow mouse or other small mammal.

A quick animal living on the shortgrass prairies, the swift fox is capable of running down its prey. Reaching speeds as high as 25 miles per hour, this small predator feeds on rabbits, ground squirrels, and mice as well as insects and some plants. The fox relies on darkness to hide from its prey, hunting at twilight or in the complete black of night.

Prairie falcons also depend on speed to catch their prey. These relatives of the peregrine fly faster than almost any other bird, and they swoop down from low, quick flight to snatch ground squirrels and birds. The prairie falcons eat far fewer birds than the peregrine do, and far fewer insects than their relative, the kestrel. Kestrels are dazzling little birds, pale blue and reddish brown in color. They hover over the ground like hummingbirds, then drop, often to eat a grasshopper.

The critical need, wherever ferrets are released back into the wild, is a healthy prairie dog population. Ferret biologists say they also need a minimum of ten separate places in which they can roam—big chunks of ground with natural prairie habitat. Ferrets, like other animals, must establish separate populations. Scattered populations are able to adapt to a greater variety of conditions. The breeding of individuals with different backgrounds increases the chances of the entire population surviving.

Unfortunately, it is not easy to find places to reestablish ferret populations. Not everyone is happy about the prospect of having ferrets or their prey for neighbors. Because prairie dogs are still killed in many states (with the support of state and federal agencies in many cases) ferrets are deprived of a vital source of food.

However, a few other release areas have been established in addition to the Shirley Basin where the first captive ferrets were set free. One is located in southern Phillips County in Montana. Once home to migrating bison herds, this area contains 26,000 acres of prairie dog towns. Fortunately, a large section of it is public land, since few private landowners are supporting plans to protect prairie dogs and reintroduce ferrets.

It is often the case that private landowners do not want to help endangered species in their areas because the presence of these animals is a nuisance to them. But unless we want to totally destroy our already-rare wildlife, we will have to become neighbors with animals like the ferret. Since opposition exists in all states where ferrets will be released, government officials need to hear from you. Money is needed to raise the ferrets in captivity, and moral support is needed for efforts to reintroduce the captive animals back into the wild.

Write to your congressional representatives, urging them to support ferret captive-breeding programs. Also write to the governors of Montana, Wyoming, South Dakota, and Colorado, asking them to protect ferret habitat—prairie dog towns—in their states, which are critical for the ferrets' future survival.

Lesser Prairie Chickens

With their floppy head feathers and large feathered bodies, lesser prairie chickens should probably be called "turkey bunnies." Many biologists, fearing for the lesser prairie chickens' future, have wanted to rename the birds, too. They'd like to give them a more distinct name, such as "prairie grouse," since chicken, to most people, is only found at the grocery store and is not much to get excited about.

Like bison and prairie dogs, the lesser prairie chicken was once very abundant in the United States. Unfortunately, they are fairly tame and easy to kill, and people liked the taste of them. The birds were shot by the thousands, and their habitat was gradually destroyed. Today the lesser prairie chickens are gone from much of their former range. They do not migrate as they once did, sweeping across the prairies in great flocks, moving north and south with the seasons. Instead, they live in small pockets of prairie, isolated from one another and unable to mix together as in times past.

The loss of genetic memory, or diversity within a given species, concerns biologists. Animals need to be different from one another in order to withstand changes in the environment. Like lures in a fishing tackle box or colored T-shirts in your drawer, differences make life more interesting. But in the natural world, diversity actually makes life possible.

The prairie chicken has lost its genetic memory of migration. This is a warning to biologists that things are not well, and the future of these beautiful birds hangs in the balance. Populations have declined steadily; as many as 10 out of every 100 birds have vanished since 1900. The area within which it lives has shrunk to about 8 percent of what it was in the 1800s.

The prairie chicken persists today in small parts of Texas, Colorado, Oklahoma, New Mexico, and Kansas. The biggest problem it continues to face is the loss of its prairie habitat. The conversion of prairie to cropland has eliminated most of its range.

New irrigation methods, especially the huge circular systems known as center-pivot sprinklers, have taken away dry sandy prairie areas that were once safe for the chickens. This kind of irrigation harms the entire ecosystem. For example, the Arkansas River in eastern Colorado and Kansas flows through former prairie chicken habitat. Now that irrigators draw water from the river, the prairie has been converted to crops. So much water is taken from the Arkansas that it frequently becomes completely dry, and some sections of the river actually have been converted to cornfields.

How do we talk people into saving birds like the prairie chicken and habitat like shortgrass or sandy prairies? Should we perform dances like those the birds do each year to call attention to their plight?

The dance of the prairie chicken—or "turkey bunny stomp," as it has been called—is a wondrous sight. Males gather each spring to perform for the hens. Traditional dancing grounds known as leks are the special stage. The birds circle, stomping, their stiff feathers raised on the back of their heads. Then they jump up in the air, calling in a stream of cak, cak, caks. They raise their brows, painted as if with mascara, and stare at one another. The orange line painted just beneath the eye matches the rising sun. Then they puff, blowing air into thin-skinned air sacs on the side of their necks. The sacs billow like a frog's croaker. The dancing and calling may attract females, who choose from among the males for mates.

Dancing, stomping, and kicking dust in the morning air, the prairie chickens perform their ancient ritual as they have for centuries. But how long will we give them room to dance?

Bison

The great bison herds of the past no longer sweep across the prairie, but the animals do remain in our midst. Some live in wild herds, while others are raised on farms like cattle and sold for their meat.

In the mid-1800s, there were approximately 60 million bison in the United States. Between 1850 and 1880, more than 75 million bison hides were sold on American markets. The killing of large numbers of bison in this way was a staggering loss for the Native Americans living on the prairies.

The bison sustained Pawnee, Comanche, Sioux, Kiowa, Blackfeet, Shoshone, Crow, and other people for many centuries. One of the most poetic accounts of the relationship between bison and people was written by N. Scott Momaday. In his book *The Way to Rainy Mountain*, he traces the history of his people, the Kiowa. He explains that the bison were not just a source of food but were connected to every aspect of Kiowa culture. When the Kiowa lost the bison on their traditional prairies, they lost much of what had sustained them as a people. Destroying the bison and its habitat was like burning down churches and grocery stores in a town. Many people who relied on bison in the 1800s starved and died. Today, the destruction of bison herds weighs on the American conscience. It is difficult to separate their killing from the deaths of Native Americans who depended on the herds, using bison hides for winter robes, lodge coverings, clothing, and more. Even the bones were used for tools.

Contemporary ranchers are just beginning to appreciate bison, though perhaps not as fully as Native Americans once did. They are now raising them because they are a leaner source of protein and because they are much gentler on the land than cattle.

Some of the most fragile spots on the prairie are trampled badly as cattle graze. This is especially true along streams, where grassland habitat meets the water. Known as riparian habitat, this precious and narrow strip of land keeps streams healthy and provides valuable wildlife living space.

Riparian habitat filters pollution and sediment, protecting the quality of water in streams and wetlands. Its dense grasses and other plants are essential to animals. Ducks, geese, sand-

LITTLE DUCKS ON THE PRAIRIE

Baby mallards, baby pintails, baby wigeon, and fluffy little cinnamon teal like to swim with their beautifully feathered parents. Many ducks are born on the prairie, nested in the grasses and wildflowers. Almost all of them are born near wetlands, though, especially those small and widely scattered wet areas that are woven into prairie landscapes.

Wet places on the prairie add diversity and new life to the grassland. Ducks are a major part of the spring and summer burst of prairie life. A thin but rich line of green plants that have adapted to having their roots in the water surrounds prairie wetlands. The plants offer shelter for duck nests and are an important food source for the many ducks that eat seeds.

Unfortunately, thousands of acres of prairie wetlands have been lost because of clearing, filling, and plowing as well as draining. With them have gone thousands of prairie ducks and other wetland birds.

People have tried many ways to protect these valuable prairie wetlands. One simple way you can help is to support the Migratory Bird Conservation Fund. This fund was established in 1934 and, together with congressional support, the money has acquired more than 3.5 million acres of wetlands. To contribute to the fund, visit your local U.S. Post Office and buy a Duck Stamp. You get a beautiful, collectable stamp, and the ducks get some new wetland homes on the prairie.

hill cranes, blackbirds, rails, and other birds build nests there and feed there, too. Generally, the riparian area is used twice as much as that of surrounding prairie. Livestock, however, trample it so badly that stream channels lose their former shape. Banks erode, fall into the stream, and turn water to mud.

Where livestock trample stream banks, it takes a great deal of work to repair the damage. Usually, the best solution is to fence the riparian areas so that the animals can't get to that land. Wild hoofed animals such as bison don't spend as much time in riparian areas. Because bison prefer to wander along streams and then leave, ranchers who have replaced cattle with bison, notice improvements in the stream and riparian habitat.

Bison have few natural enemies; however, one bison predator is the grizzly bear. Grizzlies once stalked bison on the prairies to the east of Yellowstone National Park and the Rocky Mountains. The bears, which were very large and incredibly strong, were able to take down adult bison weighing 2,000 pounds. Now that they've lost much of their open prairie habitat, it is difficult to say if the grizzly will ever be seen there again. It is also questionable whether bison, other than those living on private ranches, will ever roam free.

Even within Yellowstone, bison are held captive. During the winter, they try to move out of the park as snowfall and cold weather force them to look for better feeding grounds. But bison are said to carry a bacterial disease known as brucellosis, which can be transmitted to cattle. Ranchers outside the park do not want their herds infected, and therefore many shoot the intruders. In the winter of 1988—89, more than 500 bison were killed. Fortunately, some landowners near the park do not mind the bison and allow them to roam freely.

For centuries, bison could move up into the mountains of Yellowstone, then roam down into lower valleys during winter.

Unfortunately, we do not design our parks to fit the needs of all the animals. Bison require access to thousands of acres surrounding the park. If they had it, the true shortgrass prairie habitat would come to life again.

Wouldn't it be wonderful to see animals roam freely as they once did, even if in only one valley? This is the goal of several groups who purchase winter habitat for wildlife. Knowing that parks such as Yellowstone are not big enough to keep animals alive over long periods of time, they work to save habitat surrounding the parks. For information on how you can help protect the winter habitat of Yellowstone animals, write to the Greater Yellowstone Coalition, P.O. Box 1874, Bozeman, Montana 59771.

Mountain Meadows and Sage Grasslands

High in the western mountains, where trees can no longer grow because of lack of water, mountain meadows stretch up the slopes to form the rubies, emeralds, and sapphires of the grassland world. Covered with snow for much of the year, these meadows burst with color when spring finally arrives in the high country. Lupine, shooting stars, avalanche lilies, and marsh marigolds blanket the low-growing vegetation with blossoms. Elk graze here and give birth to their calves. Black bears and grizzlies emerging from hibernation graze on the grasses, tearing up the ground in search of tender roots or chasing down ground squirrels. Golden eagles soar overhead. Mountain goats and mountain sheep also roam these meadows. The goats climb high into the rocks above the meadows, too, reaching the highest and steepest points on the mountain slopes.

Mountain meadows—often called alpine meadows—form in thin soil above the tree line, the point at which trees can no longer grow. The meadows can exist at different elevations. In the coastal mountain ranges, some are as low as 3,000 feet above sea level. In the Rockies, alpine meadows begin forming at 6,000 feet or higher. Factors such as snowfall, soil, temperature, and moisture affect the heights at which the meadows will grow.

CHEATGRASS INVADER

One of the most successful invaders in our nation, cheatgrass has spread itself around without drawing much attention. Now covering a million or more acres in the West, cheatgrass has replaced native grasses in sage grasslands. It is also a major competitor of wheat in agricultural areas such as eastern Washington.

Cheatgrass is a relative of wheat, probably brought to our country with wheat seeds more than 100 years ago. Once introduced into the sage grasslands, cheatgrass spread quickly. This invasion was helped by the fact that ranchers were overgrazing the natural grasses. Cattle hooves pounded the soil and reduced growing ability for native species such as bluebunch wheatgrass. The wheatgrass disappeared, but the cheatgrass kept expanding its territory. Today, the dominant grass throughout much of the sage grassland states is the invader, cheatgrass.

These meadows would seem to have plenty of water since a lot of snow falls in the mountains. On Mount Rainier, for example, there may be 12 or 14 feet of snow covering the meadows in March. But in the summer months, when the snow disappears, and temperatures become quite warm, there is little moisture. Since the soil is thin and rocky on the tops of mountains, water usually trickles down the slopes into the valleys below. Large plants such as trees cannot survive these conditions, so meadow grasses and wildflowers dominate.

On the eastern slopes of the coastal ranges as well as on both sides of the Rockies, another type of grassland spreads for miles. Sage grasslands cover endless stretches in the area known as the Great Basin, especially in Nevada, Utah, and southern Idaho. Also present in eastern Oregon and Washington, these extensive sage grasslands are probably the least changed of any in the United States. They are also home to wild horses that still roam wide expanses of the West.

Sagebrush is a shrub with silver green leaves and tough, silverish branches. In some regions where it dominates the landscape, sage is removed and the land is irrigated, though much of this area is too dry and hot for agriculture. Grass and wildflower densities may be lower because of the dry conditions, but sage grasslands are spectacular when in bloom. In spring, balsam root sends up its sunflower blossoms to paint bright yellow beneath the silver green sage. Then, later in the summer, blue lupine blossoms seem to mirror the sky.

Sage grasslands often intermingle with other habitats, marching up mountain slopes to meet the high-elevation alpine meadows. They wrap in and around pine forests, forming important feeding areas for mule deer, elk, and pronghorn. As with other habitats, it is difficult to separate where one type begins and the other takes over. This is especially true when you watch how animals move back and forth between sage and forest. Both habitats are essential for the survival of many animals.

Pronghorn

Swift is the word that most comes to mind when describing the pronghorn. If the Olympics allowed animals into running events, the pronghorn would bring lots of medals back home to hang on the sagebrush. Capable of speeds above 55 miles per hour, the pronghorn is our fastest mammal. It lives in shortgrass and midgrass prairies as well as in deserts.

In sage grasslands, female pronghorn give birth to their wide-eyed young and nurse them among the tall sage plants. When a mother pronghorn moves away to feed, she leaves her baby tucked in the safety of the sagebrush. The young pronghorn will remain so still that it hardly looks as if it's breathing.

19

Sage is a major food of the pronghorn as well as other woody plants such as rabbitbrush. They also like to eat buffalo grass, wheatgrass, snowberry, grama, and a number of wildflowers. The cactus, prickly pear, and other succulent plants (those that store water in their stems and leaves) can provide all the water a pronghorn needs in dry parts of its range.

Like the bison, pronghorn populations declined tremendously during the last century. There were millions of them in the United States 150 years ago. Today however, there are only about 500,000. Domestic cattle and sheep affect the pronghorn population by grazing their areas so heavily that the pronghorn loses significant habitat. This is especially true in winter when the pronghorn needs more food to make it through the cold months.

Although coyotes prey on young pronghorn, human hunters are their major predator. The pronghorn need space to run, since quick flight is their best defense. When frightened, they call to one another with a sound more or less like a sneeze. In fact, their Klamath Indian name, Cheooh, sounds just like this call of distress. They also flare the white hairs on their rump, as if to raise a flag for others to see.

Golden Eagles

Soaring out from a steep rock cliff, a huge bird flaps, then holds its wings outstretched. Its head reflects the sunlight. Golden brown feathers give way to a darker brown body. It is probably searching for a ground squirrel.

Golden eagles live in mountainous areas as well as on the lower-elevation prairies. Although they prefer open country, they will nest in trees. The golden eagle was more common in the eastern parts of North America prior to prairie destruction but has been reduced in range over the past century. It is now most common in Rocky Mountain states.

Male Bighorn

Greater Prairie Chicken

Mullein

Opuntia polyacantha

Fireweed

WILDLIFE KIDS ON THE PRAIRIE

When children are born, they have lots of ways to get the food, warmth, and shelter they need. Hospitals, friends, and relatives care for the infants. Parents can buy what they need at the local grocery store and clothing shop. On the prairie, however, life is a little harder—especially if you are not a human.

Prairie grasses are not as protective as trees. The winds blow colder. Snow falls without a tree shield. Rain hits the ground with great force.

Birth on the prairie is tough.

Amazingly, a little more than 100 years ago, 20 million baby bison were born on the prairie every single year.

The large numbers of wildlife babies born on prairies each year help keep the populations steady. Some die, some become food for predators, some move into new areas to start another community.

Even more than forest animals, prairie wildlife need protection from people, dogs, and other unnatural intruders. If a bird nests in a tree, it is probably safe from people walking under the branches. But birds that nest on the open prairie have no place to hide. A dog's nose could easily locate a nest of babies on the ground.

Natural defense strategies exist to help the prairie kids survive. Some animals, like the pronghorn, are born with no odor. Ground-nesting birds are less colorful than those that live in trees. Small mammals of the prairie can dig burrows to escape predators.

Some prairie birds have adapted to life on the ground by developing more quickly than tree nesters. Born to run, many of them can jump from the nest soon after birth. For example, a sharp-tailed grouse can fly briefly at about ten days old. It takes a golden eagle almost three months to fly.

The golden eagle eats rabbits, ground squirrels, and prairie dogs. They fly high above, swooping down on their unsuspecting prey, reaching for it at the last moment with their strong, sharp talons. This hunting scene is one of the most exciting in nature. With powerful wing beats, they lift back into the sky and fly with their catch to a safe place for feeding.

The eagles often live in rock cliffs, building a nest of sticks tucked in crevices and on ledges. The female lays one or two white eggs speckled with brown, gray, and reddish brown markings. When the eggs hatch, the young are downy white.

Eaglets spend more than two months in the nest. Raising more than one is a tough job because of the limited supply of food. It is so hard, in fact, that if two eaglets hatch, one of them often dies. When they are about two months old, they begin to jump around on the nest, exercising and spreading their wings. Both parents will bring food to them until they are able to fly on their own. They begin to fly at about two and a half months, but it takes a good three weeks longer for them to gain the strength for full, long-distant flight. It takes many more months to learn the skills of ground squirrel catching.

Because golden eagles do eat an occasional lamb, some ranchers are not always happy to see them on their land. Other ranchers try to attract the golden eagle, knowing that it consumes large numbers of ground squirrels and prairie dogs. This predation helps keep small-mammal numbers in balance. Ranchers in open country with no cliffs or trees have been building golden eagle nesting platforms.

In many ways, people are competitors of the eagle. We may not eat ground squirrels, prairie dogs, and other small mammals, but we do take them away from the eagles. When we kill ground squirrels and prairie dogs, we intrude into the golden eagle's world in the worst possible way. Killing without consuming violates a very basic rule in nature, and people are the only ones who do this.

You can attract golden eagles to your area by making sure that small-mammal populations remain healthy. This means poisoning or shooting programs to eliminate ground squirrels or prairie dogs from prairie habitat should be banned. When you let people know how valuable small mammals are to eagles, you may change some of the attitudes that allow people to violate nature's rules. Only then will the balances needed in the eagle's world return.

Mountain Bluebirds

From Mexico to Alaska, mountain bluebirds, looking like turquoise stones springing to life, leap up from mountain meadows. The sky blue males are among our most beautiful birds, but the females are dazzling, too. Their wings are tinged with blue, and their breast feathers are a subtle cinnamon color.

Mountain bluebirds travel beyond the mountain meadows of the high Rockies, far out onto the prairies. They are common in the sage grasslands and wherever good nesting habitat is available. Their most important needs are an open feeding area and a very special kind of nesting site.

Bluebirds like to be in open country. They fly out into meadows, hovering over the ground and swooping down to snatch beetles, grasshoppers, and many other kinds of insects. But they must have sheltered nesting places. The bluebirds prefer tree cavities, such as old woodpecker holes, but they also will use nest boxes and holes in fences.

Found only in the West, mountain bluebirds never have and never will live east of Nebraska. As the West was settled and fences were strung across the prairies, bluebirds extended their natural range. Like freeways the fence lines led these

23

birds down into the valleys as they used the posts and openings for nesting. Today, instead of fence posts, miles of bluebird boxes have been used to encourage the birds to move into new areas. In many regions of the West, there are trails of these boxes with more than a thousand nests.

Not enough information exists to know for certain how healthy the bluebird population was in the past. However, it has increased in recent years, thanks to so many helping hands. If you live in the West, you can help mountain blue-birds, too. Build a bluebird nesting box, or join others to put up a trail of boxes. For nest box construction plans and information on group efforts, write to the North American Bluebird Society, P.O. Box 6295, Silver Spring, Maryland 20906-0295. They can also give you information on two other bluebirds—the eastern and western.

Grizzly Bears and Wolves

The vast open prairie landscapes spreading out to the east beyond the massive Rocky Mountains are beautiful to see. When the sunflowers are in bloom, a golden glow lights the distant ground. Pronghorn still run. Meadowlarks still sing. White-tailed deer still leap with their flag tails waving. Prairie chickens and prairie dogs may not be as abundant, but they are here. Even the black-footed ferret, rarest of all mammals in our country, is still home on the prairie. Two noticeable members of the prairie community are missing, though. And they are perhaps two of the most incredible and majestic animals.

You will have to search hard and climb high into the mountain meadows to find them. They are the wolf and the grizzly. Once at home on the prairie, they both vanished as guns, plows, and hostile people drove them up into the most remote high country. We have allowed them homes only in distant places.

Grizzlies seem to be faring better than wolves, living in diverse regions of the West. They feed in the high meadows of Yellowstone and Glacier National parks, as well as in the North Cascades of Washington State, the Selkirk Mountains of Idaho, and the Cabinet Mountains and Selway-Bitterroot Range along the Idaho-Montana border. This is not to say that the grizzlies are fine—their current mountain homes are widely separated from one another. No freeways or bike paths connect the grizzlies in one homeland to another. Human activities on the open shortgrass prairies and sage grasslands between many of the places where grizzlies now live make it almost impossible for them to move into new areas.

Contributing to their limited numbers is the fact that grizzlies do not reproduce at a rapid rate. In fact, female grizzly bears don't become mothers until they are between five and eight years old. That seems young if you think in human years, but grizzlies don't live as long as we do. The chances of a grizzly cub surviving to be an adult are only 20 to 50 percent! Their populations are so small that even a single grizzly death should be mourned. Yet people shoot grizzly bears, and do everything they can to keep them from becoming neighbors.

Attitudes about bears must change to help save them. One thing you can do is to be aware of grizzly bear needs when you travel in their mountain meadows. Several million people visit grizzly country each year, though only a handful are lucky enough to see a bear. If you hike in backcountry where grizzlies live, make sure to secure your food. Follow the recommendations of park and forest service handouts available at trailheads.

You can also help grizzly bear survival by encouraging the protection of habitat outside the national parks where the bears now live. The expansion of parks would be a great effort for people to begin now, since this kind of project would take a lot of time to succeed.

You might start your "save-the-bear" campaign in Yellowstone. More than 250 grizzly bears live there, but they need a tremendous amount of habitat outside the park, too. In fact, an estimated 60 percent of the habitat critical to grizzlies is on national forest land. You might try to persuade the federal government to protect this land for the grizzlies.

Yellowstone is also a good place to start a save-the-wolf effort. Currently, there may be only one wolf, a single wolf first seen in the park in the summer of 1992. Without these predators the ecosystem is incomplete. Because wolves travel more widely than grizzlies do, they can slowly return to areas like Yellowstone where they have been formerly wiped out.

Wolves were more common in Yellowstone about 60 years ago. They have been shot, poisoned, trapped, and chased out of most other prairie habitats. A few live in the northern mountains of Montana, Idaho, and Washington, and about 1,200 in Northern Minnesota. Like all large animals, they need lots of space to live. But lack of space is among their biggest problems. When wolves try to return to places we took from them, we shoot them. Wolves are also not welcome in our national parks where surrounding landowners object to their presence. As more people learn about these wild dogs, however, they seem to be taking their side.

The reintroduction of wolves may take place in several areas if enough people support it. Currently, the U.S. Fish and Wildlife Service is writing a plan for the reintroduction of wolves to Yellowstone. Once it is complete, the Secretary of the Interior will make a final decision on their return to the park. Help influence that decision by writing to the Secretary of the Interior. Write also to people helping the wolf: For information contact the Predator Project, P. O. Box 6733, Bozman, MT 59771.

Don't let your campaign stop at pen and paper, though. Encourage others to write. Make wolf posters. Perform wolf howlings, the music of wolf country. This is a wonderful chance to bring back one of the prairie animals most endangered by our actions, and one most likely to be saved by our concern.

Mixed Prairies

The mixed prairie, also called the midgrass prairie, stretches eastward beyond the shortgrass prairie. The mountains are distant from the edges of this region known as the Great Plains. Running like a belt down the middle of America, the plains states include the Dakotas, Nebraska, Kansas, Oklahoma, and parts of north central Texas. This big chunk of landscape still has some natural prairie left, but much of it is gone.

Less rain falls here than in the tallgrass prairie regions to the east, and the soil is not as rich. The grasses grow to be two to four feet tall, and wildlife is surprisingly abundant— at least, it was in the past. Here and on the shortgrass prairies to the west, bison populations reached their greatest numbers. Grizzly bears, wolves, and elk also roamed the mixed prairies.

During the 1930s, mixed grass prairies in Texas and Oklahoma were plowed so extensively by farmers that when drought struck, the soil started to erode. The dirt blew up during windstorms and swirled in increasing clouds of blinding dust. These disastrous storms continued to sweep across the plains, and farm after farm ceased to operate. The country was in the Great Depression, and people fled their homes in caravans, moving westward from this area that became known as the Dust Bowl.

WHY SAVE THE WILD GRASSES?

What's so good about grass, anyway? Why should we care about our native prairie grasses? They aren't as pretty as wildflowers, and a lot of them produce pollen that makes people sneeze. Even so, wild grasses are among the most valuable plants on earth.

Oats, wheat, and barley are all grasses. Without them, we wouldn't have cereal, bread, cake, doughnuts, pizza, cookies, pie, or crackers!

Native grasses are eaten by elk, bison, deer, bighorn sheep, and many other animals. Their seeds are food for birds. Their roots hold the soil, preventing erosion.

Some scientists are experimenting with wild grasses to discover mixtures that farmers will not have to plow. This would help prevent soil erosion, lower the cost of producing food, and provide a better farm environment for wildlife. This is especially true for grass crops that can be grown without expensive plowing.

But even if a grass crop is found, wild grass is still necessary to genetic diversity in nature. As if preserving family memories, each wild grass seed contains the genetic material—the genes—that enables it to grow and survive over time. Since genes in no two seeds are alike, they are sprinkled about in many, many grass plants. We must make sure that all of the genes are preserved to hold on to those many individual plants.

A devastating time, the Dust Bowl years climaxed a long history of people abusing the land. Soil was plowed during dry years, and no plants could grow to hold it in place. Suddenly, this area where millions of bison had lived in harmony with the land for centuries was reduced to dust. People had to learn through very hard times that they must listen to the land.

Dominant native grasses in the mixed prairie include big and little bluestem, often with buffalo grass growing beneath these taller plants. Western wheatgrass also grows here as well as many trees, especially along the many rivers and streams that help create habitat diversity on the open prairie.

A long list of wildflowers spreads color through the prairie grasses, including black-eyed Susan, larkspur, aster, butterfly weed, sunflower, sego lily, blazing star, and prairie rose.

Far more of this landscape is covered with wheat, corn, and other agricultural crops. Fortunately, farmers have learned to practice soil conservation, and the Dust Bowl memories loom in everyone's mind. However, there is still no widespread effort to maintain an intact section of mixed grass prairie in its natural state—at least, not one large enough to maintain all of its original wildlife inhabitants.

Some of the most spectacular wildlife that do remain in this region are those needing the wetlands scattered throughout the prairie. Beaver, otters, and fish depend on rivers and streams, while others, like nesting ducks and geese, use small prairie ponds known as potholes. These tiny wetlands once dotted the land like freckles on a nose or stars in the sky. Like the soil that was so abused during the Great Depression, wetlands have also been abused, and many prairie potholes no longer exist. More than 50 percent of the nation's wetlands have already been destroyed.

Prairie chickens, prairie dogs, and other small mammals of the shortgrass prairie find homes in the mixed grass prairies, especially in the western edges of the plains. But the biggest challenge for the future is to restore some of the larger mammals to this region. More important, it is critical to protect the populations of wildlife that still remain, such as those that dance each spring in their prairie homes.

Sharp-tailed Grouse

Spreading its wings and pointing its tail skyward, the male sharp-tailed grouse struts a dance each spring with others who have gathered on the dance floor. They stomp their feet and rattle their tails, shaking them back and forth so that their feathers click like the sound of fingers snapping. The male grouse may stop if a female approaches. He'll stand cool and composed, even bowing as an introduction to his mate.

But the sharp-tailed grouse has lost much of its dance floor—the prairie habitat—especially in the southern edges of its midgrass prairie range. Tiny islands of habitat are becoming surrounded by ever larger chunks of developed land. The grouse are gone from Oklahoma, Kansas, and much of Colorado and North Dakota. The loss of prairie grasses is blamed for most of the decline.

While sharp-tailed grouse can be found in open prairies, they prefer areas with some tree cover. They like to eat the buds of trees such as willow and aspen. This is important food in the winter when they also eat buds of serviceberry, chokecherry, and mountain ash. During warmer months, their diet includes grasshoppers, clover, and many kinds of seeds.

You can help the sharp-tailed grouse and other prairie dancers by calling attention to their habitat needs. Plant some prairie grasses, then harvest your seeds to share with friends. Maybe you could also be the first to help reintroduce these prairie birds to states where they have vanished. For starters, you can write to the governors of Oklahoma and Kansas. Maybe they don't even know the sharp-tailed grouse exists. Shouldn't they?

Sandhill Cranes

One of the places most important to the survival of the sandhill crane is a section of the Great Plains—right in the middle of America. These tall prairie dancers need wetlands as well as prairies, so each year they gather in great numbers at the Platte River in Nebraska. It is here that they descend to earth with a loud, rattling call of spring.

From wetland to prairie, sandhill cranes are wanderers. Like people, they occupy a fairly diverse homeland. They might munch on a mouse in a dry grassland, then eat a frog down by the marshy riverbank. It is up on the "back porch of their home"—the drier prairie—that you just might be lucky enough to see the cranes dance.

Long-legged like the tallest of American basketball stars, the sandhill jumps up, flaps its wings, and rattles its bill. Their clacking sound will tell you that spring is here, and the sight of their flocks descending along Nebraska's Platte River will, too. The sandhill cranes like to travel together, and they spend winters as far south as Mexico. In spring they fly north to nesting grounds. During migration, almost all of the sand-hills that spend winters east of the Rockies stop for a break along this river. Unfortunately, the sandhill has lost much of its wetland breeding habitat elsewhere in the prairies.

You can read more about sandhill cranes in the wetlands book in this series. But the most important thing you should note is that sandhill cranes need healthy wetlands scattered throughout the prairies to aid in their migration. By protecting prairie wetlands, you can help the cranes and many other animals, too.

If your family owns a farm, ask them to mow wide around small wet areas of ground, even if they don't have standing water in them. Plant willow, aspen, or cottonwood trees along streams and irrigation ditches. If you attend school in a Great Plains state, try to organize a sandhill crane festival, cele-brating the return of these prairie dancers each spring. By restoring and protecting wetlands and small streams, you might help the sandhill cranes to nest once again in places they have left.

Bighorn Sheep

Unlike the other species we are endeavoring to save, the bighorns that once lived in the northern reaches of the Great Plains can no longer be saved. Known as the Audubon bighorn, this subspecies was driven to extinction in 1910. Shot like so many thousands of other prairie wildlife, the Audubon bighorn shared the Dakota grasslands with elk, bison, and pronghorn.

You need to travel west to find other subspecies of bighorn sheep, though many of them have not fared well either. Scattered herds still live in states with shortgrass prairies and sage grasslands. By observing them, you will see long-established behavior. Much of it has to do with survival skills, including those that older males pass along to younger males.

Old males are the ones you have probably seen on television, crashing their heads together. For most of the year, they use their massive horns affectionately, rubbing against one another like a cat rubbing your leg. This behavior is actually a survival skill for the sheep. The scent on their bodies is rubbed onto the horns, then onto other bighorns. Everybody gets the same odor—kind of a group perfume. This perfume is handy in the dark or when snow blinds the eyes. Sheep can follow their leaders by sniffing the air. They can also smell an approaching stranger during the night. A friendly odor must be welcome to a bighorn living in a land of cougars and grizzly bears.

Appropriately named, bighorn sheep have enormous headgear. These trophy horns are worn by the biggest and oldest males, the ones who know most of the secrets of the land. The old males know the route from a good place to spend the summer to a safe wintering ground. Younger males do not have this knowledge and must follow the older males' leads. When hunters kill the old males for their highly prized horns, entire herds may be lost.

The grasslands where bighorns still roam need to be protected from hunters. In some regions such as Oregon and Montana where bighorns once lived, wildlife agencies have successfully reestablished new populations. This may be possible for the Dakotas, even though the Audubon bighorns are extinct. You can help by reading field guides to local mammals, finding out where bighorns lived in the past. Then contact a local wildlife agency to encourage the protection and reestablishment of new populations in areas where they have vanished.

Black-tailed Prairie Dog

Male Bison

Prairie Rattlesnake

Monarch Butterflies

Grasshopper

Prairie Sunflower

Tallgrass Prairies

A sea of waving wildflowers, the tallgrass prairie is what most people imagine a prairie to be. It is a spectacular landscape, though it is the least common kind of prairie. Tallgrass prairies cover parts of Wisconsin, Minnesota, Missouri, Illinois, Kansas and Ohio as well as most of Iowa and Indiana. The eastern fringes of the mixed grass prairie, or Great Plains states, also support stands of tallgrass prairie. Sadly, the tallgrass prairie in this country is nearly all gone.

Farmers have converted so much of this habitat to corn and soybean fields that remnant patches of tallgrass hold on only in small areas of land such as cemeteries. Fortunately, some large areas remain for us to visit and to imagine what the prairies must have been like in the past. The most extensive is the Flint Hills in Kansas. The Konza Prairie Research Natural Area, also in Kansas, is almost 13 square miles of original, undisturbed prairie. Not far from the town of Manhattan, Kansas, this is a great place to experience the tallgrass in spring. Here you can listen to the small prairie birds and watch one of the most characteristic birds of the tallgrass, the greater prairie chicken.

Many animals associated with the prairie do not roam this habitat, mainly because the grasses grow too tall. For instance, prairie dogs and pronghorn never lived in the tallgrass prairie.

WHERE HAVE ALL THE PRAIRIES GONE?

Tallgrass prairies have vanished more completely than any other major habitat in our country. Plowed under to make room for farm crops, the prairie grasses and wildflowers disappeared quickly with the settlement of the Midwest more than 100 years ago.

The remaining tallgrass prairie sleeps, as if waiting for a new century. The land could easily return to prairie once again. This is already happening at a slow pace where people replenish native plants in their former homelands.

You can restore a piece of the past, too. Search for pieces of the old prairie, collect some seeds, and plant them in an undisturbed area. Imagine the tallgrass plants spreading across the distant horizon and think of each one as if it were a redwood tree or giant sequoia. Every gentle blossom and grass stem is like a tree in a forest, holding the community together to form a piece of prairie. Hook enough of these pieces together, and you can create something wonderful.

Although bison did wander through here, they were far more abundant in the wide-open plains to the west. Elk did live in the tallgrass, but they have been hunted and killed at the same rate as their habitat has been disappearing.

Today, small patches of tallgrass prairie are scattered throughout the midwestern states, but they are much too small to support herds of large mammals like elk. Illinois, for example, once had 4,000 times more prairie than it does today. Even if its remaining 10 square miles of tallgrass were all in one location, that spot would be a tiny fraction of the area needed to create a good home for elk. In contrast, Yellowstone National Park covers more than 2,500 square miles, and the elk living there still wander from its boundaries. It takes a lot of land to sustain populations of large mammals over time.

One of the prairie's best friends is fire. You would think fire would destroy all of the grasses, but the majority of prairie plants have much longer roots than they do parts above ground. The fire burns only a current season of growth. More important, it burns plants that are invading the prairie, including trees that would overshadow the grasses and wildflowers. It is important for people to realize that fires are vital to prairie health and that they should not rush to extinguish them.

The other friend of tallgrass prairie is the person wanting to restore this devastated habitat. A prairie saver can follow the path of others who have tried for many years to re-create prairies. For example, Aldo Leopold created a prairie that you can walk through today at the University of Wisconsin at Madison. Establishing a prairie is more or less like planting a garden, and most of what you plant are flowers. You can even collect seeds from the wild. Keep them cool all winter and then sow them in spring within an area that has been tilled. Don't worry if it takes a while to create your prairie. The restored tallgrass in Wiconsin took about 50 years to complete.

WHY FARM THE PRAIRIE?

Farmers settled in the flat open spaces of the Midwest to grow corn and other crops. The main attraction of the prairies was the soil.

Forest soils can be farmed, but the topsoil—the rich layer of earth where minerals and other nutrients are available for plant growth—constitutes only 20 to 50 tons per acre. In contrast, prairie soils within the tallgrass region often contain as much as 250 tons of topsoil per acre. With five times the growing ability, the prairie soils were just what American farmers needed.

At first it was very difficult to farm tallgrass areas. Native plants grew so well that they formed an almost unbreakable layer of sod. A tough tangle of roots and shoots prevented plowing until the invention of a plow sharp enough and strong enough to break through the sod. By the year 1840, farmers owned these plows, and the tallgrass prairies began to vanish.

Greater Prairie Chickens

Like the sharp-tailed grouse and lesser prairie chicken, the greater prairie chicken is a dancer in the spring. But its habitat has been so thoroughly destroyed that populations have severely declined. These beautiful birds are gone from Ohio, Iowa, Kentucky, Texas, and Arkansas as well as their former range in Canada. In Indiana, a sad census traces their disappearance. In 1942 there were approximately 400 males, while that number declined to 4 in 1966 and to zero by 1979.

Scattered populations exist today in the northern reaches of the tallgrass prairie states, but the main center of its existence lies within Kansas. One way to help greater prairie chickens is to restore natural prairies and to encourage states to protect the birds. You might want to write to the governor of Kansas, congratulating the state for leading the way in saving prairie chickens and tallgrass prairies.

Wildflowers

Sunflowers, blazing stars, butterfly weed, and prairie clover are among the 200 wildflowers native to the tallgrass prairies. More varieties of flowers than grasses dot the prairie, and when they blossom, the world brightens. While some of the wildflowers are scattered beneath the taller grasses, others loom much higher. The compass plant, for example, shoots up as high as 12 feet with its large blossoms.

Before we plowed the prairie, people relied on prairie plants almost as much as the prairie animals. Native Americans used them for medicine and food, and some people continue to use them today. Wild onions can be found in native prairies, and you can transfer them to your own garden. Known as "yellow eyes" to the Pawnee Indians, sunflowers are also great for your garden. Plant them, eat their seeds, and spread them in fields to help re-create more natural prairie habitat. The sunflower is also a valuable food source for many birds and small mammals.

The sunflowers we grow today have been cultivated by Native Americans for a few thousand years. They raised the plants, selecting for large seeds each season. This led to an increase in the size of the average sunflower. In fact, today's seeds are about 1,000 percent larger than the wild sunflower seeds of the past.

Jerusalem artichokes, relatives of sunflowers, have also been grown for many centuries by Native Americans. The fat roots that look like potatoes are edible, though they are not highly prized for human consumption. *Liatris*, commonly known as gayfeather, is also an edible plant, but you have probably seen it used more often in bouquets. The beautiful purple flowers grow on a stalk, holding tight to the main stem.

The many prairie wildflowers native to tallgrass states are so beautiful, why plant anything else in your garden? Gay-feathers, sunflowers, coneflowers, and asters are as wonderful as any exotic flowers. Ask your parents if you can plant a prairie garden. You can order seeds and plants from many sources, including Prairie Nursery, P.O. Box 306, Westfield, Wisconsin 53964.

To learn about endangered prairie plants in your state, contact a natural resource agency, native plant society, or local National Audubon Society group. They may lead nature walks into existing prairies and will know how you can help efforts to protect wildflowers. You can also write to the Center for Plant Conservation, P.O. Box 299, St. Louis, Missouri 63166. This nonprofit organization is dedicated to conserving rare and endangered plants of the United States, including those of the prairie.

Trees

Trees on the prairie? Yes, and plenty of them. The original tallgrass prairies were not only bordered by trees, but they were sprinkled throughout like chocolate chips in a cookie. Like the chocolate, they melted into the very nature of the surroundings and offered important wildlife habitat. Even the greater prairie chickens spent a lot of time in trees, especially in oak woodlands where they could eat the acorns.

Too many trees, however, destroy the prairie, and natural prairies were always protected from this by wildfire. Today, people often manage prairies with fire to reduce or eliminate tree cover, ensuring that a few remain. The mixture of trees and tallgrass is especially common on the eastern edges of the prairie. For example, in Ohio, oaks, hickory, and hazelnut trees intermingle with grasses and wildflowers.

Providing a popular people food, hazelnuts are great trees to grow in your own prairie. They are small trees in which birds may nest, and their nuts and buds are eaten by many animals, including prairie chickens, sharp-tailed grouse, rabbits, squirrels, woodpeckers, chipmunks, and white-tailed deer.

Nuts from the hickory are also well liked by humans, making hickory a great tree to plant, too. Hickory grows much taller than a hazelnut, and its nuts are eaten by wood ducks, rabbits, squirrels, chipmunks, white-tailed deer, jays, woodpeckers, quail, and wild turkeys.

Besides being a food source, trees also provide protective cover for wildlife and a place for birds to nest. Along riverbanks, they create a significant thread of woodland in the prairie landscape. This wooded habitat breaks up the monotony of the grassland, and it is here that you will see a greater variety of wildlife than in surrounding open areas. Many animals need both the woodland and the prairie to thrive. Given the tremendous decline of our native grasslands, it is not as valuable to protect the trees without saving the grasslands, too.

It is important for people to try to restore and protect the wooded grasslands. You can begin by searching stream banks for native prairie plants, using field guides to help you identify them. Old railroad tracks often follow the streams, and it is here that many pieces of original prairie remain.

If you discover a stream and railroad bed that is bordered by prairie, declare the site a national treasure. Give the place a special name, and visit it with friends and classmates from school. Trace its history and use by Native Americans as well as the changes it has gone through over the years.

Plant trees along the stream bank, and additional prairie grasses and wildflowers if needed. Don't forget hazelnut and hickory trees if there aren't any, to provide food and shelter for wildlife. Soon your prairie will grow a woodland at its edge, and many animals will spend time here through the changing seasons.

Pacific Prairies

The prairies of the Pacific Coast are among the most strikingly beautiful grasslands anywhere on earth. They are not as well known as those farther east, probably because they are smaller. Many are actually savannahs—places where a few trees exist in harmony with grasses, such as scattered oaks surrounded by oceans of grass. These oak grasslands can be found in the San Juan Islands of Washington State, along the Columbia River in Washington and Oregon, in Oregon's Willamette Valley, and dotting the California shore.

Tucked along the ocean coast, the Pacific grasslands are home to bald eagles as well as rabbits that munch clover in the shade of the oaks. Wildflowers are scattered in the dry hills, and butterflies sip nectar or search for places to lay their eggs.

But the oak savannahs and coastal grasslands are not the only prairie habitats on the Pacific Coast. The middle part of California, especially the vast Central Valley, is the largest of the West Coast grasslands. Unfortunately, it has been altered severely since it was first settled by Europeans.

Native wildflowers still bloom in California's Central Valley, but most of the plants growing here are not those of the

45

natural grasslands. This prairie has been converted to a major western agricultural center that harvests tomatoes, lettuce, almonds, and avocados.

Since the Central Valley grasslands have been altered by agriculture, the existing wild plants are mostly annuals, meaning they live for only one season. This is in sharp contrast to natural prairies where perennials, those living for many years, dominate. The presence of annuals, which may not return the following year, creates diverse vegetation that changes over time. More moisture, cooler weather, or more sunny days help promote one plant over another.

Now that annual plants dominate the Pacific prairies, it may be impossible to restore the native prairie grasses. Even the use of fire to encourage growth of native grasses with tough, underground root systems has not succeeded in restoring prairie. One grassland near Monterey, California, has been experimentally burned and protected for more than 25 years and still has not been restored.

Western Rattlesnakes

Rattlesnakes are loved about as much as a biting dog. Unlike the dog, you can't take them to obedience school and change their nasty habits. Rattlesnakes bite. They bite to survive, and they bite in fear of humans that try anything to get rid of these beautiful reptiles.

It is no surprise that people shoot, stomp, cut, or otherwise kill rattlesnakes. They also destroy less dangerous animals for no apparent reason other than that the animals are "wild." People still don't allow the wild in their world, and the earth will not be healed until they do. All kinds of wildlife are necessary for healthy ecosystems, and all animals—including rattlesnakes—have as much right to exist as people do.

There are many kinds of western rattlesnakes—Hopi, northern Pacific, Great Basin, southern, Grand Canyon, prairie, midget faded—and the diversity is something to celebrate. The rattlesnakes have survived despite persecution, unlike other animals such as the grizzly bear. Although many kinds of rattlesnakes still exist, their range has been reduced.

You should celebrate the diversity of rattlesnakes and their ability to survive, but treat them with tremendous respect. They are highly poisonous. If you hear one rattle, stand very still until you know where it is. *Do not* jump around; just walk calmly away from the snake. Never pick one up, even if it appears to be dead.

Have you ever seen a cartoon in which an endangered animal holds a weapon to fend off an enemy? Fortunately, there are some wonderful, nonviolent ways that you can help animals like the rattlesnake. Find out as much as you can about the good things rattlesnakes do in the wild. Did you know that they prey on rodents? How many mice will a rattlesnake eat in a year? Your friends will probably be pleasantly surprised by these facts.

Predatory animals from cougars to grizzly bears, bobcats to rattlers, all have bad reputations with people. By introducing your friends to snakes, you might help them understand and appreciate predators in general.

Butterflies

California butterflies, like the native grasslands, are in trouble. Many are endangered. Two are already extinct.

The plight of California butterflies is especially severe for two main reasons. First is the widespread use of pesticides. Meant to kill agricultural pests, pesticides are really "biocides." That is, they kill *all* life, including harmless butterflies. The second threat to butterflies is destruction of their habitat. With ever-increasing human populations, Californians, for example, have spread new housing developments rapidly and in all directions, often into the coastal grasslands. Near San Francisco, the destruction of habitat was a major factor in the extinction of a butterfly called *Xerces* blue.

To ensure protection of other endangered and rare butterflies, a butterfly-conservation organization was formed that invites your participation in its efforts. Named in memory of the extinct butterfly from the California coastal region, the Xerces Society provides educational information and conducts a yearly butterfly count. You can contact them at the Xerces Society, 10 S.W. Ash Street, Portland, Oregon 97204.

Among the butterflies and moths you can search for in the California grasslands are painted ladies, skippers, swallowtails, and monarchs. The best way to encourage their presence is to protect their habitat. You can also restore butterfly habitat by planting native grasses and prairie plants.

When planting butterfly prairie plants with your friends, don't forget the needs of birds and other wildlife. Try to create areas that are as natural and complete as possible. To get ideas, visit nature preserves and use them as models for your own plantings.

One of the most famous of butterflies, the monarch, spends the winter in Pacific Grove, California. Here, it is protected by city laws, which prevent its resting trees from being destroyed. This action could be taken in other places, too. This kind of protection is especially important for monarchs since they use the same trees for many years. Keep track of where you see these beautiful, bright orange butterflies with black-bordered wings. Note the trees they use so that you can help protect them for the monarch to use again. Observe the plants the monarchs feed on in your area, such as thistle, butterfly weed, and other flowers, and plant some if there are not enough. You can also plant milkweed, which the adults use for egg laying and the caterpillars to eat as their first food in life.

Plant globe mallow for skippers, willows and birch trees for swallowtails, and hollyhocks for painted ladies. Check butterfly books for other food plants needed by both adults and caterpillars. Write to Nature Discoveries, 389 Rock Beach Road, Rochester, New York 14617, for information on obtaining butterfly eggs that you can hatch and grow.

Lawns, Gardens, and Eastern Meadows

Many old fields that were once farmed are scattered throughout the East. These open areas will, if left alone, grow back to the forested condition they once shared with the surrounding land. Cut and cleared years ago, the eastern forests have given way to thousands of acres of grassland habitats.

There are, however, natural grasslands in the East. Though they are scattered widely, they never form vast stretches of rolling prairie as they do in the West. Since they are isolated from other, more extensive grasslands, their plants are often unique to that area. They also provide homes for wildlife that require open habitat not found in the more widespread eastern forests. Eastern bluebirds, red foxes, and cottontail rabbits all benefit from the presence of these grasslands.

Where lawns and gardens blend with the surrounding natural areas, these artificial grasslands also provide valuable wildlife habitat. As discussed earlier in the book, your lawn can become even more valuable for wildlife and for the environment if you plant wildflowers and reduce the chemicals used to take care of it.

Your lawn and garden can become even more valuable if you look at your yard as a part of the larger community. Try sketching a map of your block or neighborhood, including

THE LONGEST BLUEBIRD TRAIL

Eastern bluebirds, western bluebirds, and mountain bluebirds, too —they all need nesting places that you can offer them. The birds use natural tree cavities, but if there aren't enough available, they also will nest in birdhouses.

To obtain a nesting-box building plan that is just right for the bluebirds living in your area, contact the North American Bluebird Society, P.O. Box 6295, Silver Spring, Maryland 20906. Ask them if any bluebird trails have been started in your area. If so, join them. If not, begin a trail of your own with friends and neighbors. Maybe you will build the longest trail in the world!

One trail in the grasslands of eastern Washington has more than 2,000 bluebird boxes. A trail in Canada covers more than 2,000 miles. It will be a challenge to match those efforts. If you do try, remember to take into consideration the needs of the birds. Bluebirds like to nest away from one another; they fight if they're too close. Place your boxes about 500 yards apart.

Build your birdhouses approximately four or five feet from the ground. The top of a fence post is just the right height, and using them will save you the extra work of building posts. Pastures or old fields lined with fence posts are great bluebird habitat. A trail that runs through farming country will help attract the birds. It will also make farmers happy since the birds are big insect-eaters.

all the trees and lawns. Include shrubs as well as any streams or other natural features that are good wildlife habitat.

Now take a look at your lawn and garden in relation to the surroundings. Does everyone have the same mixture of lawn, trees, and garden? Are there any natural features less common or even missing? Does everyone mow lawns right down to the ground level? If any habitat features are lacking, try to incorporate them into your own yard. Plant a few more trees, let the grass grow taller, and plant some wildflowers in an area that is not to be mowed.

Try to work together with other kids and adults in your neighborhood, creating a community wildlife area. One way to begin is to work with others to build homes for bluebirds.

Eastern Bluebirds

Once near extinction, the eastern bluebird is one of the great comeback stories of all time. People caused the decline of the birds, but they also brought them back, celebrating their return.

Eastern bluebirds like to have a few trees in their habitat, but they love meadows and other open grasslands. They used to nest in tree holes almost exclusively, but because so many trees have been cut down, these nesting sites have become scarce. Nesting habitat areas have also been sprayed with chemicals that have reduced the bluebird's source of insect food.

Bluebirds are coming back to many areas since people have started building nest boxes to replace tree nesting sites. The bluebirds will nest anywhere—a backyard or school yard—as long as they sense it is safe. The best news is, many people build more than just one box. In Canada, there is a trail of bluebird boxes that extends for more than 2,000 miles. Maybe you could start a trail that is longer yet, creating the longest trail of bluebird homes in the East.

Sunflowers

There are dozens of different kinds of sunflowers, and dozens of birds and other animals that feed on their plump, abundant seeds. There are many ways you can help spread these beautiful and valuable plants.

Planting sunflowers is as easy as placing their seeds in a bird feeder. Finches, grosbeaks, cardinals, chickadees, squirrels, chipmunks, and more will feast on your offering. As they run or fly from the feeder, they will carry seeds along with them, dropping some as they go. Seeds also will fall from the feeder, scattering on the ground.

If you can persuade your parents not to mow the sunflowers as they sprout, you can help create a small prairie in your own backyard. As the plants grow, they will become a place where birds can perch. The beautiful blossoms will paint your yard golden. Soon, the seeds will turn from a soft, pale, creamy color to a hard-shelled black. The life cycle continues, as birds feast on the seeds and drop a few. Pick them up, save them for next year, and plant them once again. Your sunflower field can spread farther and farther each year, creating a trail of golden plants for birds, chipmunks, and people to enjoy.

Not all that long ago—about 150 years in the past—the American prairies must have seemed as much a part of the world as a mall, the freeways, or your school seem today. For many people, the prairie was life itself. But all that changed very quickly in one of the most devastating acts of habitat change on our planet. With plows and farming practices of every kind, we changed the prairies to croplands or places to graze our cows and horses.

Native prairie plants still exist, however, and you can help restore prairie habitat, even if it is only in the smallest corner of your yard or school grounds. That is the beauty of life— it can be brought back from almost total elimination. Plant a seed. Grow a prairie.

As you have discovered in this book, some of our prairies, especially the shortgrass regions in the Rocky Mountains, still maintain lots of wildlife. These western areas are becoming populated quickly by people who are replacing the grizzly bears, wolves, and other animals. So, these are also the places that need your help immediately. In 150 years from now, the prairies will be much different. It is up to you to decide if those differences are beneficial.

Plant prairie seeds. Plant ideas that will help the wildlife of the West. Restore prairie habitat and work for a healthier future. And as you do, imagine the prairies of the past. They were once an incredible and a very healthy ecosystem that supported people, bison, wolves, grizzly bears, and a sea of wildflowers unlike any on earth. Perhaps you cannot re-create that image. But try. Maybe you can.

Grizzly Bear

Male Pronghorn

Burrowing Owl

Gray Fox

Coyote

Afterword

Some of the most important prairie-saving projects are happening right now on school grounds across the country. Kids are planting wildflowers and gradually watching their small gardens take on the appearance of wild prairie—especially in those areas they never weed!

Maybe these individual efforts will not restore the once magnificent grasslands in the heart of our country. But they may give people new ideas that can lead to larger prairie restoration projects. You must realize that if you plant a prairie today, it may not be big enough to welcome the bison back home. It may not become the place where prairie dogs and ferrets return, either. But it will—no matter how small it is—attract butterflies and birds.

Other people may even be inspired enough by your work to plant prairies of their own. Together, your efforts may result in the growth and spread of a much larger grassland.

When bison and black-footed ferrets first began to disappear, it would have been wonderful if people had learned from their mistakes and acted quickly to save what was left of the small prairie gardens. It would have been nicer still if people had had the vision to protect all of the vast prairie and its wildlife treasures. An important challenge for you is to share your vision, to urge others to turn lawns, gardens, and unused farmland into natural prairie once again. You can help adults by finding seeds for them, remembering to choose native wildflowers and native prairie grasses. Start with a small corner of your yard and see how it blooms. Remember, too, that the many endangered faces in the prairie need your help. Some live far from your home, but you can adopt their needs and share your concerns about them with others. Any help you can offer is important to the health of our planet. We have only One Earth. It and the future of our prairies are in your hands. It is up to you to save and share in that future.

Author's Note

My grandfather taught me more about wildlife and wild places than anyone else. His father came to this country from Switzerland, and they first settled on the prairies of Iowa. Later, they moved up to Saskatchewan, and it was there my grandfather saw his first sign of bison. This was in 1904. He did not see a live buffalo. He saw skulls and trails carved into the prairie by countless bison feet.

When my great-grandfather was young, the bison were still present—some 60 million on our prairies. In contrast, there are currently about 1 million wildebeests in Africa. But in one generation—from my great-grandfather's day to my grandfather's childhood—Americans killed all but about 1,000 of the bison. In the same time period in the late 1800s, we destroyed most of the prairies.

What will my grandchildren not be able to see in their lifetimes that I now see in abundance? What if all the geese, ducks, or squirrels were killed? What if all the bears, deer, and sandhill cranes were shot?

I am happy to know young people who are concerned about the future. I know your generation cares a great deal about wildlife and wild places. Maybe you will be the ones to encourage the restoration of prairies instead of the continuing destruction of our past. Maybe you will restore wildlife to its former habitat. Maybe you will bring bison back to my grandfather's prairie home. I hope so.

Index